CAFES & RESTAURANTS

A Linha d'Agua	3
Bela Ipanema	8
Bica do Sapato	12
Botequim do Rei	5
O Centinho do Rato	7
Casanova	19
Centro de Arte Moderna	1
Consttrada	11
Deli Deluxe	20
Eleven	4
Os Tibetanos	10
Piranha	14
Portugália	6
Ribadouro	9
Versailles	2

ACCOMMODATION

13ª da Sorte	M
Alegria	H
Amazónia	E
Avenida Alameda	I
Britania	G
Dom Carlos	K
Dom Sancho I	T
As Janelas Verdes	R
Lapa Palace	N
Lisboa Plaza	L
NH Liberdade	D
Miraparque	P
Portuense	B
Pousada de Juventude	A
Real Palácio	F
Ritz Four Seasons	C
Sana Classic Rex	O
Suíço Atlântico	J
Veneza	S
York House	

BARS & CLUBS

Armazem F	21
Estado Líquido	15
A Ginginha	12
Kapital	18
Kremlin	16
Lux	13

2

TABLE OF CONTENTS

INTRODUCTION

Lisbon, Portugal's biggest capital city, is among Europe's most historic and picturesque towns. It's situated at the confluence of the Atlantic and African continents, on the banks of the Tagus River. Lisbon is a city of contrasts, where modernism and history, tradition and creativity, culture and environment cohabit. Lisbon is a city of light as well, with its glittering river, vibrant architecture, and bright weather. Lisbon is a city full of activity, with a thriving nightlife, exciting events, and kind locals. Lisbon is a city of love because of its fascinating music, intimate cafés, and picturesque scenery.

WELCOME TO LISBON

Welcome to Lisbon, one of Europe's oldest and most intriguing towns, as well as Portugal's capital and biggest city. Lisbon is a city of contrasts, where the old and the new, customs and creativity, history and culture all live together. Lisbon is known as the city of light because of its almost constant sunshine, which reflects off the vibrant buildings and the Tagus River. Lisbon is a charming city with charming districts where you may stroll along the winding streets, take in the breathtaking vistas and landmarks, and socialize with the kind locals.

Everything you need to organize the ideal vacation to Lisbon in 2024 is provided in this book. You'll learn about the top attractions, such as modern technology, Parque das Nações, the energetic Rua Augusta, the famous Belém Tower, and the magnificent Lisbon Cathedral. This city's history, customs, and culture will also be covered. It has been molded over centuries by the impact of many civilizations, including the Portuguese explorers, the Romans, the Moors, and the Phoenicians. Aside from the nightlife, which provides a wide range of entertainment and enjoyable activities, you will also get acquainted with the local cuisine, which is abundant in seafood, pastries, and wine.

You will be fascinated by Lisbon's beauty, variety, and energy. Lisbon offers a variety of experiences, including adventure, cultural immersion, and restful getaways. Prepare to discover and delight in the delights of this magnificent city. This is your Lisbon travel guide for 2024.

TOP 10 REASONS TO TRAVEL TO LISBON

Lisbon is the only place to search for a holiday with everything you want. Here are a few reasons for your immediate travel to Lisbon:

1. Discover Lisbon's rich history and culture. Lisbon has a history spanning over 3,000 years, making it one of the oldest cities in the world. The city's monuments, museums, and districts glimpse the lives and legacies of the Romans, Moors, Christians, and Jews. Lisbon's distinctive architectural designs, including the Manueline,

Baroque, and Pombaline, are worth admiring. Indulge in Lisbon's intellectual and creative culture as well; this city gave birth to well-known people like José Saramago, Fernando Pessoa, and Fado singers.

2. Enjoy Lisbon's mouthwatering food and wine. Lisbon is a culinary lover's heaven, offering a wide range of delicacies that capture the complexity and diversity of Portuguese cuisine. Savor the delectable pastries, spicy cheese, juicy meat, and fresh seafood Lisbon offers. Lisbon's magnificent wines, which include the crisp and refreshing Vinho Verde and the sweet and fortified Port, are also available for tasting. In the city's eateries, cafés, and bars, you can enjoy the welcoming and energetic ambiance while mingling with the people and hearing their tales.

3. Explore Lisbon's breathtaking natural splendor. Lisbon is fortunate to have a stunning natural environment with views of the river, hills, and ocean. While unwinding, you may stroll in the fresh air in Lisbon's verdant parks

and gardens. In addition, you may go to Lisbon's neighboring beaches and islands to sail, swim, surf, and sunbathe. Dolphins, flamingos, cork trees, and orchids are just a few of the fauna and flora you may enjoy in Lisbon.

4. Experience Lisbon's happiness and bustle. With a lively and varied nightlife to suit every taste and mood, Lisbon is a city that never sleeps. In Lisbon's hip clubs and discos, you may dance the night away while listening to the newest songs or the classic Fado. Lisbon's theaters and concert halls provide a variety of live music and comedy acts, including both local and international performers. You may also participate in Lisbon's joyous and vibrant festivals, such as the Carnival, the Feast of St. Anthony, and New Year's Eve.

5. Shop till you drop at the markets and boutiques of Lisbon. Lisbon is a shopping haven, offering various choices to suit every taste and budget. Wander around the stores and booths in Lisbon's quaint and ancient markets to

discover everything from fresh vegetables and flowers to antiques and handicrafts. Lisbon's stylish stores, which feature the newest styles in clothing and design, are another place to spoil yourself. In Lisbon, you may also haggle at the flea markets and outlet stores to obtain fantastic bargains and savings.

6. Visit Lisbon's museums and other attractions to learn and enjoy. Lisbon has plenty of chances for you to study while having a good time. You can visit Lisbon's museums and galleries to see the art, historical, scientific, and technological collections. In addition, you may explore Lisbon's sites and attractions, which include the Jerónimos Monastery, the Tower of Belém, and the Castle of São Jorge. You may visit theme parks and amusement parks in Lisbon to enjoy the games, rides, and entertainment.

7. Relax and pamper yourself at Lisbon's spas and wellness centers. There are plenty of ways to unwind and treat yourself in Lisbon. You may use treatments and therapies that revitalize your

body and mind by visiting Lisbon's spas and wellness facilities. In addition, you may go to Lisbon's thermal and mineral springs and bathe in the curative waters, which can help your skin and muscles. You may also go to Lisbon's yoga and meditation centers to practice the poses and methods that will soothe your emotions and soul.

8. Meet and interact with the friendly and hospitable people of Lisbon. Lisbon is a nice city that offers visitors a wide grin and open arms. You may socialize and engage with Lisbon's warm and welcoming residents, who will make you feel like a member of their family. Portuguese, one of the world's most widely spoken and exquisite languages, is another language you may study and practice. Lisbon's storied past and rich cultural traditions are also available to learn about and enjoy.

9. Travel to and from Lisbon efficiently and economically. Traveling to and from Lisbon is convenient and reasonably priced. Lisbon is easily accessible from the rest of Portugal and

Europe by car, rail, bus, or airplane. Lisbon has a well-developed public transportation system that allows you to go about the city via bus, cab, metro, tram, or tramway. Because Lisbon is a small, walkable city, you can also get about on foot, by bike, or by scooter. Lisbon offers various lodging choices, from cost-effective hostels and guesthouses to opulent hotels and apartments.

10. Make full use of your Lisbon time and budget. Lisbon provides excellent value for both your time and money. Lisbon has plenty of activities for all tastes and events so that you can make the most of your time and finances there. Walking tours, street art, concerts, and festivals are free or inexpensive events and activities in Lisbon. Lisbon offers many additional savings opportunities, including city cards, passes, and coupons.

CHAPTER ONE

BEST 20 THINGS TO DO IN LISBON 2024-2025 (WITH PHOTOS, ATTRACTIONS, SIGHTSEEING, LANDMARKS & INSIDER TIPS)

Lisbon is a city that appeals to all visitors, including those seeking entertainment, culture, history, or the outdoors. These 20 top Lisbon activities are sure to make your vacation memorable.

1. Belém Tower

One of Lisbon, Portugal's most recognizable sights is the 16th-century Belém Tower, a UNESCO World Heritage Site. Built as both a ceremonial entrance to the city and a defensive structure, it is a prime example of the distinctive Manueline architectural style, which blends Moorish, Gothic, and Renaissance features. You can explore the tower's five floors, which include the King's Chamber, the Chapel, and the Terrace, where you can take in expansive views of the city and river, or you can admire the tower's exterior, which is decorated with elaborate carvings, turrets, balconies, and a rhinoceros gargoyle.

Address: Ave. Brasília, Portugal, 1400-038 Lisboa

Prices vary from €6 for individuals to €3 for elderly and students. Children under 12 and the first Sundays of each month are free.

Hours of operation: Mondays and certain holidays closed; 10 AM to 5:30 PM, October to April; 10 AM to 6:30 PM, May to September

2. Jerónimos Monastery

One of Lisbon's most striking landmarks, Jerónimos Monastery, is another UNESCO World Heritage Site with Manueline architecture. It was constructed in the sixteenth century to honor the Portuguese explorers' journeys of discovery, and some of the most well-known Portuguese historical personalities, like Vasco da Gama, Luís de Camões, and Fernando Pessoa, are buried there. You may explore the inside of the monastery, which houses the beautiful Church of Santa Maria, the abbey, the refectory, and the marine museum, or you can marvel at the intricate façade of the monastery, which is adorned with statues of saints, monarchs, and mythological animals.

Address: 1400-206 Lisboa, Portugal; Praça do Império

Prices vary from €10 for individuals to €5 for seniors and students. Children under 12 and on the first Sunday of each month are admitted free.

Hours of operation: Mondays and certain holidays are closed: 9:30 AM to 6 PM in May and 9:30 AM to 5 PM in October and April.

3. Portas do Sol Miradouro

One of Lisbon's top vistas is Miradouro Portas do Sol, where you can take in breathtaking views of the city's winding streets, colorful buildings, the Alfama neighborhood, and the Tagus River. It is situated on a terrace next to the statue of Lisbon's patron saint, St. Vincent. It has a café where you may have wine or coffee while taking in the view. You may also explore the underground tunnel underneath the Terrace, which has several cartoon paintings that creatively and amusingly narrate Lisbon's history.

Address: 1100-411 Lisboa, Portugal; Largo das Portas do Sol

Price range: Free

Hours of operation: 24/7

4. Castelo de São Jorge

Lisbon's most visited site is the ancient castle, Castelo de São Jorge, perched above the city. Throughout history, it has functioned as a royal house, a military castle, and a jail. The Moors constructed it in the eleventh century and

subsequently captured it by the Christians in the 12th century. You may tour the museum, the archeological site, the gardens, and the peacocks that wander the castle grounds or stroll around the walls and towers, which provide breathtaking views of the city and the river.

Address: R. de Santa Cruz do Castelo, Lisboa, Portugal, 1100-129

Price range: €10 for adults, €5 for pensioners and students, and €0 for kids under 12

Hours of operation: March through October, 9 AM to 9 PM; November through February, 9 AM to 6 PM.

5. **Praça do Comércio**

Lisbon's main plaza, Praça do Comércio, is among Europe's biggest and most exquisite. It was constructed in the eighteenth century to represent the riches and might of Portugal after the catastrophic earthquake that destroyed much of the city in 1755. The area has a huge arch, a statue of King José I, and a mosaic pavement. Yellow buildings with government offices, museums, and cafés border it. The area also serves as the entry point to the Tagus River, from where you may see the city from a new angle by taking a sailing trip, a cruise, or a ferry.

Address: Praça do Comércio, 1100-148 Lisboa, Portugal.

Price range: Free

Hours of operation: 24/7

6. Santa Justa Lift

Santa Justa Lift, one of Lisbon's most recognizable icons, is a distinctive and attractive elevator that links the city's upper and lower regions. It was constructed in the 19th century in the neo-Gothic style using wood and iron by a student of Gustave Eiffel, the engineer who created the Eiffel Tower. You may ascend to the top of the lift for a panoramic view of the city and the river, or you can take the lift to Carmo Square, where you can explore the remains of the Carmo Convent.

Address: R. do Ouro, Lisbon, Portugal 1150-060

The price range is €1.50 for a single journey and €5.15 for a circular trip; public transit passes are free.

Hours of operation: May through October, 7 AM to 10:45 PM; November through April, 7 AM to 9 PM.

7. **Pastéis de Belém**

Lisbon's most well-known and delectable pastries are pastéis de Belém, and everyone visiting the city should taste them. These are flaky pastry custard pies with a creamy interior, dusted with sugar and cinnamon. They are available in numerous bakeries and cafés across the city and are best enjoyed warm and fresh. The Pastéis de Belém factory and café, which has been in operation since 1837 and employs a family-secret recipe that has been handed down through the generations, is the only location where the original and genuine pastéis de Belém are created. The pastries are available for purchase at the counter, or you may eat them while sipping tea or coffee inside the café.

Address: R. de Belém 84-92, Lisboa, Portugal 1300-085

Price range: €1.20 per pastry

Hours of operation: Sunday through Thursday, 8 AM to 11 PM; Friday and Saturday, 8 AM to midnight

8. LX Factory

Located in the Alcântara neighborhood of Lisbon, LX Factory is a creative and cultural center housed in a former industrial complex. It's a location where you can discover everything from literature, fashion, music, art, and food in one area. In addition to attending the regularly scheduled events, seminars, and concerts, you may explore the galleries, studios, stores, and restaurants in the former factories and warehouses. A few of the LX Factory's main attractions are the bookstore, the rooftop bar, and the enormous typewriter. You may also take in the street art and graffiti that adorn the walls and buildings.

Address: R. Rodrigues de Faria 103, 1300-501 Lisboa, Portugal

Price range: Free

Hours of operation: 6 AM to 4 AM daily

9. Oceanário de Lisboa

One of the finest things to do in Lisbon with kids is to visit Oceanário de Lisboa, the biggest and most popular aquarium in Europe. Showcasing the richness and beauty of marine life from all seas and locations of the globe, it is situated in the futuristic and sophisticated Parque das Nações, an area constructed for Expo 98. More than eight thousand creatures and plants, such as sharks, rays, penguins, otters, jellyfish, and coral, may be seen in four distinct ecosystems that symbolize the Antarctic, Pacific, Indian, and Atlantic seas.

Address: Lisboa, Portugal; Esplanada Dom Carlos I, s/nº, 1990-005.

Price range: €19 for adults, €13 for children and seniors, free for children under 3

Hours of operation: 10 AM to 8 PM from July to September, 10 AM to 7 PM from October to June

10. Tram 28

Experience Lisbon like a native with Tram 28, a classic yellow tram that passes through some of the city's most picturesque and historic areas. The tram takes around forty-five minutes to complete, and you may get on and off at any of the stations. Along the route, you can visit some of Lisbon's top attractions, including the Sé Cathedral, Estrela Basilica, Alfama, and Graça. Along with taking in the city and river sights, you can also experience the nostalgia and beauty of the vintage tram.

Address: Several locations throughout the city

Price range: €3 per ticket, free with a public transportation pass

Hours of operation: 6 AM to 11 PM daily

11. Sintra

One of Lisbon's greatest day outings is the fairytale village of Sintra, which is around 30 kilometers away from the capital. A UNESCO World Heritage Site, it is well-known for its wacky and charming gardens, castles, and

palaces nestled within the verdant hills and woods of the Serra de Sintra. Some of Sintra's most notable sights are open for you to see, including the National Palace, the Moorish Castle, the Pena Palace, and the Quinta da Regaleira. Additionally, you may stroll about the town's quaint, colorful streets, home to various stores, cafés, and eateries.

Address: Portugal's Sintra

Price range: Depending on the attraction, prices vary from €8 to €14 for adults to €6.50 to €11.50 for elderly and children.

Hours of operation: 9:30 AM to 6 PM or 10 AM to 8 PM, depending on the attraction

12. Cascais

A fantastic day excursion from Lisbon is to the beach resort of Cascais, which is only 30 kilometers away from the capital. It was once a fishing hamlet but gained popularity as a retreat for Portuguese nobility and monarchy, and it has managed to hold onto its elegance and charm. You may sunbathe, swim, surf, or sail on Cascais's sandy beaches and crystal-clear blue seas. Additionally, you may explore Cascais's historical and cultural landmarks, including the Paula Rego Museum, the Santa Marta Lighthouse, and the Cascais Citadel. Further, you may stroll around the marina's shops, eateries, and promenades.

Address: Portugal's Cascais

Price range: Free

Hours of operation: 24/7

13. MAAT

The Museum of Art, Architecture, and Technology, or MAAT for short, is one of Lisbon's most cutting-edge and modern institutions. It is situated adjacent to the Tagus River in the Belém neighborhood. It comprises two structures: a modern oval-shaped building with a contemporary design, a rooftop terrace, and an old power station displaying Lisbon's industrial past. You may visit the installations and exhibits that delve into the relationships between technology, architecture, and art concerning society and culture. You can also view the city and the river from the museum grounds.

Address: Av. Brasília, Portugal, 1300–598 Lisboa

Prices vary from €9 for adults to €4.50 for elderly and students. Children under 18 and the first Sundays of each month are free.

Hours of operation: 11 AM to 7 PM from Wednesday to Monday, closed on Tuesdays

14. **Time Out Market**

The oldest and biggest market in Lisbon, the Mercado da Ribeira, is home to the culinary hall known as Time Out Market. You can get some of the city's most varied meals and beverages under one roof. There are over forty booths and kiosks, from traditional Portuguese fare to foreign delicacies. Additionally, ice cream parlors, pubs, and cafés provide regional and handcrafted drinks and treats. Further, you may take pleasure in the live entertainment and music that the market often hosts.

Address: Av. 24 July 49, Lisbon, Portugal, 1200-479

Price range: €5 to €15, depending on the stand or kiosk

Hours of operation: Sunday through Wednesday, 10 AM to midnight; Thursday through Saturday, 10 AM to 2 AM.

15. São Roque Church and Museum

São Roque Church and Museum is a creative and religious landmark in Lisbon's Bairro Alto neighborhood. One of the few structures to survive the 1755 earthquake was this 16th-century church, regarded as one of the city's most exquisite churches. The church's interior is stunning, with paintings, gold, marble, azulejos, and other elaborate details contrasted with an austere and basic facade. Additionally, you may go to the museum, which has a collection of religious artwork, including statues, relics, and garments.

Address: Largo Trindade Coelho, 1200-470 Lisboa, Portugal

Price range: €2.50 for adults, €1.50 for students and seniors, free for children under 14 and on Sundays and holidays

Hours of operation: Tuesday through Sunday, 9:30 AM to 5 PM; closed on Mondays.

16. Fado Museum

Located in the Alfama neighborhood of Lisbon, the cradle of the ancient Portuguese music genre known as fado, is the Fado Museum, a cultural and musical destination. It is a museum that

chronicles the development of fado from its 19th-century beginnings to its current position as a representation of the Portuguese spirit and identity. Along with the histories and pictures of some of the most well-known fado singers, such as Amália Rodrigues, Carlos does Carmo, and Mariza, you can see the exhibitions and displays that include the instruments, costumes, posters, and fado recordings. Fado's songs and performances are also available for you to listen to, and you can even attempt to sing along.

Address: 1100-139 Lisboa, Portugal; Largo do Chafariz de Dentro 1, 1110

Prices range from €5 for adults, €2.50 for seniors and students, €0 for children under 12, and €2 to 6 on Wednesdays.

Hours of operation: Tuesday through Sunday, 10 AM to 6 PM; closed on Mondays

17. Tile Museum

The artistic and historical Tile Museum is located in the old Madre de Deus Convent, a 16th-century structure that was both a monastery and a hospital. This museum displays the artistry and craftsmanship of Portuguese tiles, also known as azulejos, which are ceramic tiles decorated with various colors and designs via painting and glazing. You may see the exhibition and collection of tiles that portray historical, religious, cultural, and daily situations—the tiles date from the fifteenth century to the present. The convent's cloister, choir, and chapel are also visible; they are embellished with tiles and other works of art.

Address: R. da Madre de Deus 4, Lisbon, Portugal, 1900–312

Price range: Prices vary from €5 for adults to €2.50 for elderly and students. Children under 12 and the first Sunday of each month are free.

Hours of operation: Tuesday through Sunday, 10 AM to 6 PM; closed on Mondays

18. The Gulbenkian Museum

The Gulbenkian Museum is a contemporary, green destination next to Eduardo VII Park on Avenidas Novas. It offers a diverse range of

cultural and artistic offerings. It's a museum featuring the personal art collection of Calouste Gulbenkian, a wealthy businessman and philanthropist from Armenia who gave money and art to Portugal. You may see the exhibition and collection of almost 6,000 works of art, including books, paintings, sculptures, jewelry, and furniture from antiquity to the present. In addition, you may take in the scenery and activities in the museum's theater and gardens.

Address: Avenue. de Berna 45A, Lisbon, 1067-001

Pricing range: adults €12.50, pensioners and students €6.25, children under 18 free, and Sundays free

Hours of operation: Open Wednesday through Monday from 10 AM to 6 PM; closed on Tuesdays.

19. Bairro Alto

Located in the city's higher region, Bairro Alto is a vibrant and bohemian area that offers one of the greatest views of Lisbon's nightlife. Hundreds of taverns, pubs, clubs, and restaurants can accommodate every mood or taste, from contemporary jazz venues to classic fado homes. You may socialize with the residents and visitors who swarm the neighborhood every night while taking in the music and beverages of Bairro Alto. Additionally, you may stroll through Bairro Alto's streets and alleyways, home to art galleries, antique stores, and street art.

Address: Portugal's Bairro Alto, Lisboa

Price range: varies from €2 to €20, depending on the bar, pub, club, or restaurant.

Hours of operation: 6 PM to 4 AM daily

20. Cristo Rei

One of the most striking sites in the city is the enormous figure of Christ known as Cristo Rei, which faces Lisbon on the other side of the Tagus River. Influenced by the Christ the Redeemer monument in Rio de Janeiro, it was constructed in the 20th century as a sign of faith and thankfulness. The statue lies in Almada and may be accessed by vehicle, bus, or boat. It is perched on a hill. Reaching the statue's base, 82 meters high, will allow you to take in the city and river vistas. At the top of the 110-meter-tall monument, you may ride an elevator to get a bird's-eye perspective of the surrounding area.

Address: Portugal's Alto do Pragal, 2800-058, Almada

Price range: €6 for adults, €3 for children and seniors, free for children under 6

Hours of operation: October through February, 9:30 AM to 6:15 PM; March through September, 9:30 AM to 6:45 PM

CHAPTER TWO

LISBON ESSENTIALS

Lisbon is Portugal's capital and largest city, one of Europe's oldest and most beautiful cities. With a population of around 500,000, it is situated at the mouth of the Tagus River on the Atlantic coast. For any taste and interest, Lisbon has many attractions and activities, including historical and cultural landmarks, galleries and museums, parks and gardens, beaches and islands, markets and festivals, and eateries and bars. Lisbon offers many more necessities that you should be aware of both before and during your vacation, including:

Currency: You may swap your money at the airport, banks, hotels, or exchange offices. The euro (€) is the currency of Lisbon and Portugal. Additionally, you may use your debit or credit card to make purchases or get cash out of one of the many ATMs around the city. As of January 2024, the currency rate is around 1 euro = 1.18 US dollars.

Language: Portuguese is the primary language spoken in Lisbon and Portugal, and it's a lovely, expressive language. You may demonstrate respect and interest in the local people and culture by learning Portuguese terms and phrases to facilitate communication and interaction.

Electricity: The electricity in Lisbon and Portugal is 230 volts, 50 hertz, and the plugs and sockets are type C and F, the same as in most of Europe. Adapters and converters may be required based on the devices you use and where you are from. These are available for purchase in supermarkets, electronics shops, and airports.

Lisbon and Portugal are in the same time zone as Greenwich Mean Time (GMT) and Western European Time (WET). However, WET is one hour behind Central European Time (CET). Portugal and Lisbon both use daylight saving time (DST), which causes them to advance their clocks by one hour in March and revert them by one hour in October. As of January 26, 2024, the time in Lisbon is 08:03:31.

Weather: Lisbon and Portugal have pleasant, sunny weather with an average temperature of 18°C and 750 mm of rainfall annually. With an average temperature of 11°C, January is the coldest month, while August is the warmest, with an average temperature of 24°C. With an average rainfall of 127 mm, November is the wettest month, while July is the driest with only 4 mm. When the weather is nice and there are fewer tourists, March through May or September through November are the ideal times to visit Lisbon.

LISBON FESTIVALS

Lisbon is home to several festivals that honor the customs and culture of both Lisbon and Portugal while providing a ton of fun and entertainment.

You may participate in some festivals, feel the enthusiasm and energy of the people and the city, and join in on their celebrations and festivities. Among the celebrations are:

Festas de Lisboa: This month-long celebration of the city and Santo António, its patron saint, is Lisbon's primary event. June is the festival's month, offering various events and activities, including street parties, concerts, parades, and fairs. The customary sardine BBQ, the vibrant paper decorations, and the basil plants—presented as a sign of friendship and love—are all event elements. The event, which is free and accessible to everyone, is held around the city in several districts, including Graça, Bairro Alto, and Alfama.

One of the largest and most well-known music events in Lisbon, if not the whole globe, is called Rock in Rio Lisboa. This biannual event, which happens in May or June, brings together some of the greatest and most well-known performers and bands from various genres, including rock, pop, hip-hop, and electronic. Entertainment and activities, including rides, games, stores, and food vendors, are also available during the event. Tickets for the event cost between €69 and €117, depending on the day and the lineup. It is held in the Parque da Bela Vista.

Noite Branca: This is a night to remember and one of Lisbon's most enchanted and wonderful occasions. It is a yearly festival in September and includes various artistic and cultural manifestations, including theater, dance, music, and film. The city and the monuments are illuminated and decorated by the event's abundance of lights and colors. The event, which is free and accessible to everyone, is held around the city in a variety of locations, including Baixa, Chiado, and Belém.

LISBON TOURIST SEASONS

Lisbon has many distinct tourism seasons, which change based on the temperature, cost, and volume of visitors. Depending on your interests and expectations, you may choose the ideal time of year to visit the city and its attractions. The following are a few of Lisbon's tourism seasons:

High season: The high season in Lisbon is from June to August, the most popular and crowded time to visit the city. With an average temperature of 24°C, the weather is hot and sunny, and the town is bustling with activity. The festivals and events are regular and varied, and the sights and activities are accessible. But the city may be loud and hectic, with steep costs and lengthy lines. To minimize the stress and crowds, properly plan your schedule and reserve your lodging and transportation in advance.

Low season: November through February is Lisbon's low season, making it the least congested and popular period to visit the city.

The city is peaceful and quiet, and the weather is chilly and wet, with an average temperature of 12°C. The festivals and events are few and basic, and the attractions and activities are closed or restricted. Still, the city may be quaint and pleasant, and the prices are low, and the lines are short. You can enjoy the city and its sights and activities without the crowds and trouble by finding amazing prices and specials for your lodging and transportation.

Shoulder season: March through May (or September through October) is Lisbon's shoulder season and the ideal time to visit the city. The city is pleasant and laid back, and the weather is bright and moderate, with an average temperature of 18°C. The festivals and events are reasonable and diverse, and the sights and activities are accessible. The city may be lovely and fun, the costs are fair, and the lines are tolerable. With some flexibility in your bookings, you may take advantage of the city's attractions and activities while making the most of your travel and lodging choices.

GETTING AROUND LISBON

Lisbon has an excellent public transport infrastructure that serves most of the city and its environs. Public transit is a perfect way to see the city's major regions and attractions and neighboring places like Ñbidos, Sintra, and Cascais. Based on your requirements and tastes, other possibilities include bikes, Uber, and taxis. Here are a few methods for getting about Lisbon:

Metro: With four lines connecting the city's major districts and points of interest, including the airport, the Parque das Nações, the Baixa, and the Chiado, the metro is the quickest and most convenient method to get about Lisbon. Every day from 06:30 to 01:00, the metro operates every five to ten minutes. You may purchase a single ticket, a day pass, or a rechargeable card, depending on your requirements and tastes. A single ticket costs

€1.50, a day pass costs €6.40, and a rechargeable card costs €0.50, in addition to the tariff for each journey.

Bus: With over 100 routes connecting the city and its environs, including Belém, Alcântara, Sintra, and Cascais, buses are the most convenient and comprehensive mode of transportation in Lisbon. The bus departs every day at 5:00 and returns every 10:00, at a frequency of every ten to twenty minutes. You may purchase a single ticket, a day pass, or a rechargeable card, depending on your requirements and tastes. A single ticket costs €2, a day pass costs €6.40, and a rechargeable card costs €0.50, in addition to the tariff for each journey.

Tram: With five lines connecting the city's major neighborhoods and sites, including the Baixa, Alfama, Castelo, and Graça, the tram is the most historic and quaint mode of transportation in Lisbon. Every day from 6:00 to 23:00, the tram operates at a frequency of every

15 to 30 minutes. You may purchase a single ticket, a day pass, or a rechargeable card, depending on your requirements and tastes. A single ticket costs €3, a day pass costs €6.40, and a rechargeable card costs €0.50, in addition to the tariff for each journey.

Train: Four lines leave from various stations in the city, including the Rossio, the Cais do Sodré, the Santa Apolónia, and the Oriente. The train is ideal for reaching neighboring places like Sintra, Cascais, and Óbidos. Every day, from 5:00 to 1:00, the train operates at a frequency of every 10 to 30 minutes. You may purchase a single ticket, a day pass, or a rechargeable card, depending on your requirements and tastes. Depending on the route and destination, a single ticket might cost anywhere from €2 to €10.

Taxi: With over 3,000 cars available at the airport, rail stations, hotels, and streets, the cab is the most convenient and adaptable mode of transportation in Lisbon. The taxi operates twenty-four hours a day and has a high frequency of operation. Depending on the driver's desire and availability, you can pay with a card or cash. Depending on the route and the destination, the cost ranges from €5 to €20. Additional fees may apply for weekend, night, or baggage services.

Uber: With many drivers and cars available for booking and payment via the app, Uber is the most well-liked and practical substitute for taxis. Uber operates at a high frequency, every day and every hour. Many car and service options are available, including UberX, UberXL, UberBlack, and UberGreen. Depending on the route and the destination, the cost ranges from €4 to €15. Weekend, night, or baggage services are all included in the price.

Bike: Riding a bike is the most environmentally friendly and healthiest way to move about Lisbon. Several bike lanes, bike routes, and bike stations are located throughout the city's various neighborhoods and tourist destinations, such as the Parque das Nações, the Belém, and the LX

Factory. The bike operates often, every day, from 7:00 to 23:00. Depending on your requirements and interests, you may hire a bike from bike stations, bike stores, or bike apps. Depending on the length of time and distance, the pricing range is €1 to €10.

LISBON'S TRAVEL REGULATIONS

Lisbon has several travel laws to protect locals and tourists from the COVID-19 epidemic while ensuring their comfort and safety. To enjoy your vacation and stay and keep clear of any issues or fines, you must abide by and respect the travel restrictions. The following are some of Lisbon's travel laws:

Visa: Depending on your nationality and the reason for your visit, the visa is the formal and legal license to enter and remain in Lisbon, Portugal. Lisbon and Portugal are included in the Schengen Area, which allows citizens of the 26 Schengen nations and those of nations free from visa requirements, such as the US, Canada, Australia, or Japan, to visit and remain in the country without needing a visa. If you enter the nation for travel, business, or transit, you can stay for up to 90 days total within 180 days. You must apply for a visa at the Portuguese embassy or consulate in your home country before you leave if you are not a citizen of one of the Schengen or visa-exempt nations if you want to stay longer than ninety days, or if you have another reason for visiting, such as employment, education, or family. A few papers and details are required, including your passport, vacation itinerary, lodging confirmation, health insurance, and ability to pay. Depending on the kind and term of the visa, there is a €80 application cost and a 15–30 day processing period.

COVID-19: The coronavirus-caused infectious and contagious illness that has afflicted the globe and led to several health and travel restrictions and measures. In response to the COVID-19 epidemic, Lisbon and Portugal have implemented several laws and regulations to stop the virus's spread and safeguard the public's health and welfare. Among the rules and directives are:

Testing: Regardless of your country or the reason for your visit, you must provide a negative COVID-19 test result that was obtained up to 72 hours before your arrival, as well as evidence of vaccination or recovery, to enter and remain in Lisbon, Portugal. PCR, antigen, or fast testing may be used; the choice will rely on the authorities' preferences and what is available. In addition, a passenger locator form with your travel and medical history and contact and personal information must be completed. The paperwork is available online or at the airport and must be turned in before your trip. A random test, or temperature check, may also be required at the airport based on the circumstances and the authorities' judgment.

Quarantine: Should you test positive for COVID-19, exhibit symptoms or have contact with COVID-19 cases, or originate from a high-risk region or nation like Brazil, India, or South Africa, you must quarantine yourself for 14 days at your place of lodging or a certified facility. You must monitor your health, report any changes or issues, and adhere to the guidelines and advice provided by the health authorities. After 14 days, you may terminate your quarantine if you test negative for COVID-19, do not exhibit any symptoms, and have not been in contact with any COVID-19 cases.

Mask: You must wear a mask that covers your mouth and nose in all public and indoor areas, including airports, train stations, hotels, shops, restaurants, and museums. You must also wear a mask in some outdoor areas where maintaining a 2-meter physical distance is impossible, like squares, streets, parks, and beaches. Surgical masks, FFP2 masks, or fabric masks are required based on the authorities' desire and availability. In addition, you should have an extra mask and a plastic bag for storing and discarding old masks. A mask costs between €0.50 and €2 and may be purchased at the airport, supermarkets, or pharmacies.

Social Distancing: In public and indoor areas like airports, train stations, hotels, shops, restaurants, and museums, as well as in some outdoor regions like squares, streets, parks, and beaches, where masks are not required, you must maintain a physical distance of two meters from other people. When you cough or sneeze, you should cover your mouth and nose with tissue or your elbow to prevent physical contact such as handshakes, embraces, or kisses. You should also refrain from touching your mouth, nose, or eyes with your hands and wash them often with soap and water or an alcohol-based sanitizer.

Capacity: You must adhere to the capacity restrictions that apply to certain public and interior areas, including train stations, airports, hotels, stores, restaurants, and museums, as well as some outdoor areas, such as streets, squares, parks, and beaches. The capacity limitations, which range from 25% to 75% depending on the circumstances and the authorities' judgment, are determined by the activity's size, ventilation, and danger level. In addition to waiting for your turn or purchasing a ticket if the area is full or crowded, you must obey the signs and instructions that specify the space's capacity and direction.

DOCUMENTS FOR MOVING AROUND IN LISBON

In Lisbon, several papers are necessary or advised to navigate the city, the nation, and some sites and events. You should own and carry the required documentation to prevent any issues or fines and enjoy your journey and stay. The following are some of the documentation needed to navigate Lisbon:

Your passport is the most crucial and necessary document that verifies your identity and nationality, permits you to enter and remain in Lisbon, Portugal, and allows you to travel to other nations. For the visa and stamps, you must have a valid passport with at least two blank pages that expire six months after the date of departure. In addition, you must keep a photocopy or digital duplicate of your passport and submit it to the closest embassy or consulate immediately if it is lost or stolen.

Visa: Depending on your nationality and the reason for your visit, the visa is the formal and legal license to enter and remain in Lisbon, Portugal. Lisbon and Portugal are included in the Schengen Area, which allows citizens of the 26 Schengen nations and those of nations free from visa requirements, such as the US, Canada, Australia, or Japan, to visit and remain in the country without needing a visa. If you enter the nation for travel, business, or transit, you can stay for up to 90 days total within 180 days. You must apply for a visa at the Portuguese embassy or consulate in your home country before you leave if you are not a citizen of one of the Schengen or visa-exempt nations if you want to stay longer than ninety days, or if you have another reason for visiting, such as employment, education, or family. A few papers and details are required, including your passport, vacation itinerary, lodging confirmation, health insurance, and ability to pay. Depending on the kind and term of the visa, there is a €80 application cost and a 15–30 day processing period.

Documents proving your health status—a COVID-19 test result, vaccination record, or recovery proof—allow you to enter and remain in Lisbon, Portugal, and partake in certain attractions and activities without testing or quarantine. Regardless of your country or the reason for your visit, to enter and remain in Lisbon and Portugal, you must provide documentation of your vaccinations, evidence of recovery, or a negative COVID-19 test result obtained no more than 72 hours before your arrival. PCR, antigen, or fast testing may be used; the choice will rely on the authorities' preferences and what is available. In addition, a passenger locator form with your travel and medical history and contact and personal information must be completed. The paperwork is available online or at the airport and must be turned in before your trip. A random test, or temperature check, may also be required at the airport based on the circumstances and the authorities' judgment.

Lisboa Card: This card gives you free or discounted access to more than 80 attractions, museums, and monuments in Lisbon, as well as free and unlimited use of public transportation, including the metro, buses, trams, and trains. The card comes in 24, 48, or 72-hour durations and may be purchased online or in person at the tourist office. The card may save you up to €100, depending on your spending. It costs €22, €38, or €48, accordingly. The card must be activated at the first attraction or mode of transportation you use, and it must be shown at the ticket office or entry to any other attractions or modes of transport you want to use.

Rechargeable card: These let you utilize public transportation, including buses, trains, trams, and metro, without purchasing a single ticket or a day pass each time you wish to use it. The card may be purchased at any metro or train station, kiosks, or retail stores. Afterward, it can be recharged with any money that suits your requirements and preferences. The card costs €0.50 and is good for several user travels. The card must be validated at the entry or departure of the vehicle you use, and you must use the machines or screens at the stations or stops to verify the card's validity and balance.

CHAPTER THREE

LISBON PACKING LIST: WHAT TO PACK FOR A TRIP TO LISBON

Lisbon is a beautiful and vibrant city that offers travelers a rich cultural and historical experience. It would be best to prepare wisely to make the most of your trip to Lisbon, whether for a quick weekend getaway or a longer stay. Here are some packing recommendations and pointers for a vacation to Lisbon.

Clothes: Lisbon has a moderate climate all year round, while the winters may be cold and the summers can be scorching. Packing layers you can easily add or remove based on the weather is thus advised. A few things you should always carry are:

A lightweight coat or jacket for the chilly mornings and nights

An air-conditioned sweater or cardigan for the house

An umbrella or raincoat for those infrequent downpours

For the sunny days, a hat, sunglasses, and sunscreen

appropriate footwear for navigating the slopes and cobblestone streets

Bring a swimsuit and a towel to visit the public pools or beaches.

A garment or elegant ensemble for a formal dinner or nightlife

Lisbon is a vibrant and fashionable city, so you should bring some accessories to complete the look. A few things to think about are:

A shawl or scarf to stay warm and add style to your ensemble

To keep yourself safe from pickpocketing, carry your things in a crossbody or backpack.

A smartphone or camera to record the breathtaking scenery and street art

Use a power bank or a portable charger to keep your electronics charged.

A converter or travel adapter to connect your devices

A reusable cup or water bottle to remain hydrated and cut down on plastic waste

Money and documents: Although Lisbon is a welcoming and secure city, you should exercise caution when handling your possessions and personal data. Among the things to take are:

A passport or identification card to verify your identity and get entry into the nation

If you are going from outside the EU or the Schengen region, you will need an ETIAS permit or a visa.

A health card or travel insurance to cover unexpected medical costs

A debit card or credit card to make transactions and take out cash

A few euros of cash for local businesses, public transit, or tips

A photocopy or duplicate of your identification papers and credit cards in case they are misplaced or stolen.

CHAPTER FOUR

BEST BEACHES IN LISBON

Lisbon is rich in culture, history, sunshine, and the sea. In Lisbon, several stunning beaches are conveniently accessible by vehicle or public transit. There is a beach for everyone, whether you want to spend an enjoyable day surfing, lounging on the sand, or watching a breathtaking sunset. The following are some of Lisbon's best beaches:

Carcavelos Beach: This is one of Lisbon's busiest and most well-liked beaches in the summer. It is around 20 kilometers west of the city center and takes approximately 30 minutes to get by rail from the Cais do Sodré station. The beach has waves that are good for surfing and other water activities and a lengthy expanse of golden sand and clean water. Along the seafront are several eateries, stores, and pubs. The beach is free to enter and is accessible year-round.

Guincho Beach: About 35 kilometers northwest of the city center, close to the town of Cascais, is one of Lisbon's most picturesque and untamed beaches. Buses leave Cascais station, roughly a 40-minute rail ride from Cais do Sodré station. The rocky shoreline of the beach is home to pine trees, rocks, and dunes. Perfect for windsurfing, kitesurfing, and sailing, the wind is high, and the sea is rough and frigid. Around the beach are a few hikes and overlooks. The beach is free to enter and is accessible year-round.

One of Lisbon's longest and broadest beaches is Costa da Caparica, which crosses the Tagus River and is around 15 kilometers south of the city center. From Cais do Sodré station, you may take a ferry to Cacilhas, and from there, take a bus to Costa da Caparica. The beach's more than 30 miles of sand are broken up into many areas, each with its amenities and atmosphere. Some portions are better suited for families, livelier sections, and more isolated and naturist sections. Popular activities on the beach include surfing, fishing, and sunbathing due to the quiet and warm sea. The beach is free to enter and is accessible year-round.

WHERE TO STAY IN LISBON

Lisbon is a vibrant, varied city with various areas that provide unique experiences and sights. The ideal region to stay in Lisbon will depend on your vacation choices, financial situation, and mode of transportation. The following are some of the top neighborhoods in Lisbon to stay in:

Lisbon's historical and cultural district, Baixa and Chiado, is home to several well-known sites, including the Carmo Convent, the Santa Justa Lift, and the Praça do Comércio. Along with many stores, cafés, eateries, and museums, the region is bustling day and night. This is a terrific place to stay if you want to enjoy the old town's beauty and be near the major sights. But it can also be pricey, congested, and raucous, particularly in the summer.

The oldest and most scenic parts of Lisbon are Alfama and Castelo, where you can see the real, traditional aspect of the city. The neighborhood is distinguished by its colorful homes, meandering lanes, and breathtaking hilltop vistas. Some of the most significant landmarks, including the National Pantheon, the Sé Cathedral, and the São Jorge Castle, are also located there. If you want to take in the scenery, listen to fado music, and immerse yourself in the history and culture of the region, this is a terrific place to stay. Nevertheless, it can be steep, difficult to get there by automobile, and devoid of contemporary conveniences.

Lisbon's fashionable and bohemian neighborhoods, Bairro Alto and Príncipe Real, are home to many of the city's greatest pubs, clubs, and restaurants. Along with its abundance of vintage stores, street art, and art galleries, the region is renowned for its alternative and creative atmosphere. If you want to have fun and discover Lisbon's nightlife and cuisine, this is a terrific place to stay. However, it may also be dangerous, crowded, and loud at night, particularly on weekends.

Lisbon's historic and cultural districts, Belém and Alcântara, are home to some of the city's most striking and iconic structures, including the Monument to the Discoveries, the Jerónimos Monastery, and the Belém Tower. This region has the city's greatest museums, parks, and pastry shops. This is a terrific place to stay if you want to explore the lush, tranquil surroundings and discover more about Lisbon's maritime and colonial past. It can, however, also be distant from the city core, requiring additional money and time for transportation.

LISBON'S BEST LUXURY HOTELS

Lisbon has a variety of lodging choices, ranging from upscale hotels to inexpensive hostels.

There are some of the greatest luxury hotels in Lisbon if you're searching for an upscale and exclusive place to stay. The following are a few of Lisbon's top luxury hotels:

One of Lisbon's most renowned and exquisite hotels is the Four Seasons Ritz, situated next to Eduardo VII Park in the posh Avenida da Liberdade neighborhood. The hotel has 282 rooms and suites with all the contemporary conveniences and comforts furnished traditionally but elegantly. In addition, the hotel has an indoor pool, a restaurant, a bar, a rooftop fitness center, and a terrace with expansive city views. Along with various experiences and activities, including wine tastings, culinary workshops, and art excursions, the hotel provides individualized and attentive service. A basic room costs between €500 and €800 per night.

Tivoli Liberdade Avenue Lisboa: Located next to Rossio Square in the center of the Avenida da Liberdade neighborhood, this hotel is one of

Lisbon's most recognizable and historically significant. The hotel has 285 rooms and suites that are tastefully designed in a modern, sophisticated manner and furnished with all the conveniences of the contemporary world. The hotel also has two restaurants, two bars, a spa, a fitness center, a rooftop pool, and a garden with a fountain. The hotel provides a range of experiences and activities, including shopping guides, cultural events, and city excursions, along with a skilled and welcoming staff—a basic room costs between €300 and €500 per night.

One of Lisbon's most elegant and sophisticated hotels, the Bairro Alto is situated close to the Chiado district in the bustling and trendy Bairro Alto neighborhood. The hotel exudes elegance and coziness with 87 tastefully appointed rooms and suites with all the newest conveniences. In addition, the hotel has a restaurant, café, spa, rooftop bar, and library. In addition to a range of experiences and activities, including yoga sessions, fado performances, and wine tastings, the hotel provides friendly, attentive service. A basic accommodation costs between €200 and €400 per night.

LISBON'S BEST BOUTIQUE HOTELS

Lisbon has many lodging choices, from contemporary design hotels to classic guesthouses. Some of the greatest boutique hotels in Lisbon are available if you're hoping for a more private and customized stay. The following are a few of Lisbon's top boutique hotels:

Memmo Alfama: Located next to the São Jorge Castle in the gorgeous and historic Alfama district, this hotel is one of Lisbon's most quaint and comfortable accommodations. With 42 rooms that are tastefully furnished in a minimalist and elegant manner, the hotel offers all the comforts and contemporary facilities. In addition, the hotel has a wine bar, a pool, a library, and a rooftop patio. In addition to a range of experiences and activities, including wine tastings, fado concerts, and walking tours, the hotel provides warm, responsive service. A basic room costs between €150 and €250 per night.

One of Lisbon's most wealthy and fashionable hotels is the Lumiares Hotel & Spa, situated next to the Miradouro de São Pedro de Alcântara in the hip and happening Bairro Alto neighborhood. The hotel has 53 rooms and suites that are tastefully designed in a modern, sophisticated manner and furnished with all the conveniences of the contemporary world. In addition, the hotel has a restaurant, bar, fitness center, spa, and a rooftop terrace with 360-degree city views. The hotel provides a range of experiences and activities, including yoga sessions, culinary courses, and art exhibits, together with attentive and competent service. A basic accommodation costs between €200 and €300 per night.

One of Lisbon's most charming and tasteful hotels, Santiago de Alfama, is close to the Sé Cathedral in the picturesque and ancient Alfama neighborhood. The hotel has 19 guestrooms and suites with elegant, traditional décor and all the conveniences of the contemporary world. In addition, the hotel has a restaurant, café, bar, and beauty salon. In addition to providing friendly, helpful service, the hotel offers a range of experiences and activities, including massages, city excursions, and cultural events. A basic room costs between €150 and €250 per night.

BEST BUDGET-FRIENDLY HOTELS IN LISBON

Lisbon has several reasonably priced and excellent lodging alternatives, making it a terrific place to visit for a reasonable price. There are many of Lisbon's greatest reasonably priced hotels if you're searching for an inexpensive and cozy place to stay. The following are a few of Lisbon's top reasonably priced accommodations:

One of Lisbon's most well-known and award-winning hostels, Home Lisbon Hostel is situated close to Rossio Square in the bustling Baixa neighborhood. The hostel has 24 rooms, including private and dorm-style accommodations. Each room is tastefully arranged in a bright, comfortable manner and comes furnished with all the necessities. In addition, the hostel has a lounge, bar, balcony, and shared kitchen. In addition to a wide range of events and activities, including dinner parties, pub crawls, and city excursions, the hostel provides a warm and welcoming atmosphere. Dorm beds might cost anything from €15 to €25 per night.

One of Lisbon's most up-to-date and stylish hotels is the Hotel Gat Rossio, close to Restauradores Square in the accessible Baixa neighborhood. The hotel has 71 rooms that are furnished with all the necessities and a bright, minimalistic design. The hotel also has a patio, a bar, and a breakfast area. In addition to a range of experiences and activities, including bike rentals, city tours, and cultural events, the hotel provides a straightforward and effective service. A basic room costs between €50 and €100 per night.

Situated within the Rossio train station in the heart of the ancient Baixa district of Lisbon, this hostel is one of the city's most distinctive and entertaining options. The hostel has 28 rooms, including private and dorm-style accommodations. Each room is uniquely adorned with creative accents and furnished with all the necessities. In addition, there is a garden, a lounge, a bar, and a shared kitchen at the hostel. Along with various events and activities, including yoga classes, movie evenings, and karaoke nights, the hostel provides a warm and welcoming atmosphere. Dorm beds might cost anything from €15 to €25 per night.

RECOMMENDED HOTELS IN LISBON

Lisbon has various lodging alternatives to suit multiple preferences, requirements, and price points. For your stay in Lisbon, you may choose the ideal hotel based on your tastes. The following are a few of the top-rated hotels in Lisbon:

One of Lisbon's most renowned and traditional hotels, Hotel Avenida Palace is situated next to the Marquês de Pombal Square in the classy and central Avenida da Liberdade neighborhood. The hotel has eighty-two rooms and suites with all the luxuries and contemporary conveniences in an opulent and historic design. In addition, the hotel has a restaurant, bar, lounge, and conference space. In addition to providing sophisticated and kind service, the hotel offers a range of experiences and activities, including afternoon tea, live music, and city excursions. A basic accommodation costs between €250 and €400 per night.

One of Lisbon's most practical and cozy hotels, Hotel Mundial, is close to Martim Moniz Square in the bustling Baixa neighborhood. The 350 rooms and suites of the hotel are furnished in a stylish but homey manner with all the conveniences and facilities of the modern world. In addition, the hotel has a rooftop patio, two bars, two restaurants, and a conference room. In addition to a range of experiences and activities, including wine tastings, city tours, and cultural events, the hotel provides courteous and competent service. A basic room costs between €100 and €200 per night.

One of Lisbon's most quaint and intimate hotels, Hotel Lisboa Plaza is close to the Avenida metro station in the classy and convenient Avenida da Liberdade neighborhood. The hotel has 112 rooms and suites that are tastefully adorned classically and furnished with all the conveniences of the contemporary world. In addition, the hotel has a library, fitness center, bar, lounge, and breakfast area. In addition to providing friendly, helpful service, the hotel offers a range of experiences and activities, including massages, city excursions, and cultural events. A basic room costs between €100 and €200 per night.

CHAPTER FIVE

FAMOUS LOCAL DISHES AND DRINKS TO TRY IN LISBON

Lisbon's rich and varied culinary scene results from the city's nautical and ethnic past. Lisbon and Portugal's history, culture, and topography are reflected in the available foods and beverages range. Here are a few well-known Lisbon cuisines and drinks you should try:

The most famous and mouth-watering dessert in Lisbon, if not the whole globe, is pastel de nata. This little, spherical custard pie has a crunchy, flaky crust and a creamy, sweet interior and is dusted with sugar and cinnamon. It was created in the eighteenth century by the monks of the Jerónimos Monastery, and the renowned Pastéis de Belém bakery still makes it using the same recipe. Pastry de nata is available in almost every café and pastry store in Lisbon. It is best consumed warm, along with a cup of coffee.

The bacalhau is the most adaptable and common fish in Lisbon and Portugal. It's dried and salted fish that may be prepared in many ways, including baking, grilling, frying, and stewing. In Lisbon, bacalhau à brás (shredded cod with eggs, potatoes, and olives), bacalhau com natas (cod with cream and cheese), and bacalhau à Gomes de Sá (cod with potatoes, onions, eggs, and parsley) are some of the most well-liked bacalhau meals. In Lisbon, bacalhau can be found in almost every restaurant and bar. It is often served with wine, bread, and salad.

Lisbon's most popular and traditional beverage, ginjinha, is a representation of the essence of the city. Made from sour cherries, sugar, and alcohol, it is a powerful and sweet liqueur that is matured in oak barrels. Made in the 19th century by a Galician monk, it is still served in the original Ginjinha tavern in Rossio Square. Ginjinha is a popular beverage in Lisbon's pubs and kiosks. It is often served in little glasses with or without a cherry on the bottom. In winter, it's the ideal beverage to perk you up and keep you warm.

Lisbon's most traditional and celebratory meal, Sardinha Asada, is a summertime mainstay. It is eaten with bread, boiled potatoes, and salad after the sardine is grilled and seasoned with salt and olive oil. This recipe, which highlights the freshness and availability of Atlantic salmon, is easy to prepare and delicious. Sardinha Assada is served at many restaurants and street vendors in Lisbon. It's most popular during the Santo António festival in June, when the smell and sound of sizzling sardines fill the air.

The most distinctive and refreshing wine in Lisbon, and all of Portugal, is vinho verde. Made from green grapes, it is a youthful, light wine with mild dizziness, low alcohol, and fruity taste. It goes well with salads, shellfish, and cheese. It is available in white, rosé, or red varieties. Lisbon has many pubs and stores offering vinho verde, often served cold in a tall glass.

BEST PLACES TO VISIT IN LISBON

Lisbon has various attractions, from museums and historical sites to beautiful parks and vistas, hip and vibrant districts, and marketplaces. Explore Lisbon's beauty and charm and find something to suit every taste and interest. The following are some of Lisbon's top tourist destinations:

The main gateway to Lisbon, Praça do Comércio, is the city's most magnificent and stunning plaza. Situated on the banks of the Tagus River, it is encircled by tastefully designed yellow buildings housing the municipal hall, the tourism office, and government offices. Along with these characteristics, the plaza has a mosaic pavement, a statue of King José I, and a massive arch. The plaza is a fantastic location to visit the Baixa and Alfama districts and enjoy river views and architecture.

Lisbon's most famous and significant structure is the Torre de Belém, a UNESCO World Heritage Site. Built in the Manueline style in the sixteenth century, the tower is embellished with religious and marine themes. It was once a ceremonial and defensive building that served as a jail and a customs house. In addition to offering breathtaking views of the river and bridge, the tower is an excellent resource for learning about the history and culture of Lisbon and Portugal.

Lisbon's most picturesque and historic site is the Castelo de São Jorge, a tourist must-see. This ancient fortress is perched atop the city's tallest hill, with a commanding view of Alfama and Baixa neighborhoods. The castle's history is lengthy and tumultuous, spanning the Roman, Moorish, and Christian eras. Discover the castle's ramparts, towers, and museum, and take in the expansive views of the river and city below.

Lisbon's most stunning structure is the Mosteiro dos Jerónimos, a UNESCO World Heritage Site. Constructed in the Manueline style during the 16th century, the monastery is devoted to the Order of Saint Jerome. In addition, the royal family and explorers like Vasco da Gama and Luís de Camões were buried there. The church, cloister, and museum are all worth seeing at the monastery, which is also a wonderful spot to take in the artwork and architecture.

One of Lisbon's most exquisite and romantic vistas, the Miradouro de Santa Luzia is a well-liked destination for residents and visitors. Perched atop the Alfama district's hill, it provides breathtaking views of the river, the National Pantheon's dome, and rooftops. The vantage point has a fountain, a pergola, and a tiled wall. From this perspective, you can easily visit the Sé Cathedral and the São Jorge Castle and unwind and snap beautiful images.

BEST PLACES TO EAT IN LISBON

Lisbon has an amazing and varied culinary scene, ranging from international and fusion cuisine to street food, snacks, and traditional and regional delicacies. Lisbon offers many dining options, including exquisite, sophisticated restaurants, vibrant and energetic markets, and comfortable, rustic pubs. Here are a few of Lisbon's top dining establishments:

One of Lisbon's most well-known and well-liked seafood restaurants, Cervejaria Ramiro, is a must-try for every seafood enthusiast. It is situated in the Intendente neighborhood and has a big aquarium, wooden tables, and a laid-back vibe. A large and fresh assortment of seafood, including clams, prawns, crabs, lobsters, and oysters, is available at the restaurant. As a dessert, the eatery offers the well-known prego, a beef sandwich. The restaurant charges between €20 and €40 per person and is open daily from 12:00 to 00:30.

Time Out Market is a hip and enjoyable dining destination in Lisbon that caters to a wide range of palates and price points. Situated in the Cais do Sodré neighborhood, it is a spacious and contemporary food hall with over 40 vendors serving various foods and beverages, including pastries, ice cream, foreign and fusion cuisine, and traditional and regional delicacies. The market also has a culinary school, a souvenir store, and a stage for live music. The market is open daily from 10:00 to 0:00, with prices per person ranging from €5 to €15.

One of Lisbon's most quaint and intimate dining spots is Taberna da Rua das Flores, a hidden treasure for any cuisine enthusiast. It is a little rustic bar in the Chiado neighborhood with wooden furnishings and an antique feel. The tavern serves a daily-changing cuisine inspired by Portuguese and global tastes based on seasonal and local products. The bar also provides homemade sweets and a selection of wines and beers. The tavern charges between

€10 and €20 per person and is open Monday through Saturday from 12:00 to 23:00.

CHAPTER SIX

THE BEST BARS, CLUBS & NIGHTLIFE IN LISBON

Lisbon has a thriving and varied nighttime culture, from quaint and traditional taverns to hip and contemporary clubs to energetic, colorful streets and squares. Lisbon offers several options for places to drink, dance, and enjoy yourself from dusk till dawn. These are some of Lisbon's best night spots, pubs, and clubs:

Pensão Amor: A must-visit for every night owl, this is one of Lisbon's most quaint and eccentric pubs. It is an old, restored brothel in the Cais do Sodré neighborhood. It has various rooms and themes, including a barbershop, library, lounge, and pole dancing area. In addition to a vast array of inventive drink options such as wines, gins, and cocktails, the bar hosts live music performances, burlesque acts, and poetry readings. The bar is open Monday through Saturday from 18:00 to 04:00, with drinks between €5 and €10.

Lux Frágil is a well-known and crowded club in Lisbon that is a must-visit for everyone who enjoys throwing parties. Situated in the Santa Apolónia neighborhood, this spacious and contemporary club has three stories and a rooftop patio with views of the bridge and river. The club hosts a range of events, including concerts, DJ performances, and themed parties, in addition to providing a wide and high-quality selection of music, ranging from electronic to hip-hop to indie. The club charges between €10 and €20 for admission, which includes a drink, and is open from Wednesday through Saturday from 23:00 to 6:00.

Bairro Alto: This is not a single place but a whole neighborhood and Lisbon's most lively and colorful nightlife area. Situated in the Bairro Alto neighborhood, it is a twisting labyrinth with small lanes brimming with hundreds of bars, taverns, and restaurants that suit various preferences and price points. You may enjoy the vistas and the street art in this laid-back and welcoming location while drinking, chatting, and mingling with residents and visitors. The area is open daily from 18:00 until 2:00, with drinks priced between €1 and €5.

CHAPTER SEVEN

THE MOST ROMANTIC THINGS TO DO IN LISBON

Lisbon is a city that exudes romance and charm in many forms, from its breathtaking scenery and sunsets to its warm and welcoming areas to its extensive and varied cultural heritage. In Lisbon, there are plenty of romantic activities to choose from, whether you're planning an exciting night out or a leisurely, picturesque day. The following are a few of Lisbon's most romantic activities:

Take a Ride on Tram 28: This is one of the most iconic and nostalgic ways to explore Lisbon and a perfect activity for couples. The ancient, yellow tram travels through some of the city's most scenic and historically significant neighborhoods, including Alfama, Graça, and Estrela. You may enjoy the old town's scenery and vibe by getting on and off the tram at any stop. The tram costs €3 per ticket and operates daily from 6:00 to 21:00.

Watch the Sunset at the Miradouro de Santa Catarina: This is one of Lisbon's most beautiful and romantic viewpoints and a favorite spot for locals and tourists alike. Perched atop Santa Catarina's hill, it provides an amazing view of the river, the bridge, and the cityscape below. You may enjoy live music or street performers as you watch the sunset and the lights come on from the seats or the wall. The vantage point is free to enter and open daily from 8:00 to 0:00.

Have a Candlelight Dinner at the Chapitô à Mesa: This is one of Lisbon's most charming and cozy restaurants and a hidden gem for any foodie. It is housed within the Chapitô Circus school and has wooden tables and vibrant pillows as part of its eclectic and rustic design. With a selection of wines and beverages, the restaurant serves a tasty and imaginative menu centered on Portuguese and Mediterranean cuisine. Additionally, the restaurant has a patio with a breathtaking view of the river and the castle. The restaurant charges between €20 and €40 per person and is open Tuesday through Sunday from 19:00 to 00:00.

Take a walk along the Ribeira das Naus: This is one of Lisbon's most scenic and relaxing places and a great place to enjoy quality time with your partner. This riverbank promenade runs from the Cais do Sodré to the Praça do Comércio and is lined with greenery, seats, and fountains. You may relax on the grass and have a picnic or a drink, stroll beside the lake, and take in the monuments and boats. The promenade is free to enter and is open daily from 6:00 to 0:00.

Explore the Museu do Fado: This is one of Lisbon's most emotional and cultural locations for those who like music. It is a UNESCO Intangible Cultural Heritage and a museum devoted to the fado, Lisbon's traditional and soulful music. The museum presents the fado's history and development through displays, instruments, and recordings. Every day, the museum hosts a live fado concert, including some of the top guitarists and vocalists in the city. The museum costs €5 per entry and is open from 10:00 to 18:00 every Tuesday through Sunday.

BUDGET THINGS TO DO IN LISBON

Lisbon is a very cost-effective city with many free and inexpensive things to do, see, and eat. Lisbon offers affordable entertainment options that allow you to enjoy the city's beauty and charm. Here are a few inexpensive activities you may want in Lisbon:

Explore the Free Museums and Monuments: Lisbon is home to many free museums and monuments open to the public daily or all year. In addition to taking in some of the city's most striking and significant architectural structures, you may learn more about the history and culture of Lisbon and Portugal. Among the monuments and museums that are free are:

Museu Nacional do Azulejo: This museum is dedicated to the azulejo, the traditional and colorful tile that decorates many of the buildings and walls in Lisbon. In addition to having a studio where visitors may create their tiles, the museum showcases an assortment of tiles from various eras and designs. The museum is free from 10:00 to 14:00 on Sundays and public holidays. Regular admission is €5.

Mosteiro dos Jerónimos: This 16th-century monastery was built in the Manueline style and is a UNESCO World Heritage Site. In addition, the royal family and explorers like Vasco da Gama and Luís de Camões were buried there. On Sundays and public holidays, the monastery is free from 10:00 to 14:00. Normally, a ticket costs €10.

Museu Coleção Berardo: This museum is dedicated to modern and contemporary art and is one of Portugal's most visited museums. Picasso, Warhol, Dali, and Koons are just a few of the well-known and significant artists from the 20th and 21st centuries whose works are on show at the museum. Every day from 10:00 to 19:00, the museum is free to enter.

Discover the Markets and Street Art: Lisbon is home to many free-to-explore markets and street art that enliven the city with color and personality. Many markets and street art installations can be found around the city, and you may take in the originality and variety of the regional sellers and artists. Among the marketplaces and street art are:

LX Factory: A former industrial complex, this area is now a center of the arts and culture, home to several street art installations, stores, cafés, and dining establishments. In addition to a massive mural of a woman's face by Brazilian artist Vhils, there is a plethora of street art with various styles and meanings painted on the walls, rooftops, and floors. The LX Factory is free to enter and is open daily from 6:00 to 04:00.

Feira da Ladra is Lisbon's oldest and most famous flea market and a great place to find bargains and treasures. Various items, including clothing, jewelry, crafts, antiques, literature, and street performers, are available. The Feira da Ladra is free to enter and is open from 9:00 to 18:00 every Tuesday through Saturday.

Enjoy the Free Views and Parks: Lisbon offers a lot of free parks and views full of beauty and natural elements. Numerous parks and vistas can be found around the city's hills and other regions, and you may take in the landscape and ambiance. Among the vistas and green spaces are:

Miradouro de São Pedro de Alcântara: This is one of Lisbon's most panoramic and romantic viewpoints and a great place to admire the city and the river. In addition to the many seats, sculptures, and fountains, there is a shop where you can purchase refreshments and food. The vantage point is free to enter and open daily from 8:00 to 0:00.

Jardim da Estrela: This is one of Lisbon's most beautiful and peaceful parks and a great place to relax and picnic. In addition to the several ponds, flowers, and trees, there is a playground, a bandstand, and a café. Every day from 7:00 to 0:00, the park is open. There is no charge to enter.

CHAPTER EIGHT

LISBON MONEY SAVING TIPS

Lisbon is a very affordable city, but it can be costly if you don't budget and prepare ahead. Lisbon offers great financial savings without sacrificing the quality or pleasure of your vacation. Here are a few Lisbon money-saving suggestions:

Buy a Lisboa Card: This card gives you free or discounted access to more than 80 attractions, museums, and monuments in Lisbon, as well as free and unlimited use of public transportation, including the metro, buses, trams, and trains. The card comes in 24, 48, or 72-hour durations and may be purchased online or in person at the tourist office. The card may save you up to €100, depending on your spending. It costs €20, €34, or €42, respectively.

Dine at Inexpensive and Local Establishments: Lisbon offers a wide variety of affordable and local eateries where you may savor some of the city's greatest and most genuine meals and beverages for a fraction of the cost of the upscale and touristic establishments. Numerous inexpensive and locally owned dining establishments exist throughout the city's several districts, including Alfama, Bairro Alto, and Mouraria. Several affordable and nearby dining options are:

O Trevo: This is a small and cozy tavern in the Bairro Alto area near the Praça Luís de Camões. It serves a range of appetizers and sandwiches, including the prego, a beef steak sandwich, and the banana, a pork steak sandwich. It also offers a selection of beverages, including ginjinha, wine, and beer. Every day from 8:00 to 2:00, the tavern is open. Each item costs between €1 and €5.

A Padaria Portuguesa: This is a chain of bakeries located in different areas and neighborhoods of the city, such as Baixa, Chiado, and Belém. Along with coffee, tea, and juice, it serves a selection of pastries, breads, cakes, and sandwiches. Additionally, it offers a breakfast and lunch menu with many combinations and choices. The bakery is open daily from 7:00 to 20:00, with prices per item ranging from €1 to €5.

Mercado da Ribeira: This large modern food hall is located near the Time Out Market in the Cais do Sodré area. It serves various foods and beverages, including pastries, ice cream, worldwide and fusion cuisine, and traditional and regional delicacies. It also has a culinary school, a live music venue, and a gift store. The market is open daily from 10:00 to 0:00, with prices per person ranging from €5 to €15.

Stay at Budget-Friendly and Central Places: Lisbon has a lot of budget-friendly and major places to stay, where you can enjoy comfortable and convenient accommodation for a reasonable price. Numerous reasonably priced and conveniently located lodging options are available in several parts of the city, including Baixa, Alfama, and Bairro Alto. Several affordable and conveniently located accommodations include:

Home Lisbon Hostel: One of Lisbon's most popular and award-winning hostels is located near Rossio Square in the central and lively Baixa area. The hostel has 24 rooms, including private and dorm-style accommodations. Each room is tastefully arranged in a bright, comfortable manner and comes furnished with all the necessities. In addition, the hostel has a lounge, bar, balcony, and shared kitchen. In addition to a wide range of events and activities, including dinner parties, pub crawls, and city excursions, the hostel provides a warm and welcoming atmosphere. Dorm beds might cost anything from €15 to €25 per night.

Hotel Gat Rossio: This is one of Lisbon's most modern and chic hotels in the central and convenient Baixa area, near the Restauradores

Square. The hotel has 71 rooms that are furnished with all the necessities and a bright, minimalistic design. The hotel also has a patio, a bar, and a breakfast area. In addition to a range of experiences and activities, including bike rentals, city tours, and cultural events, the hotel provides a straightforward and effective service. A basic room costs between €50 and €100 per night.

Lisbon Destination Hostel: This is one of Lisbon's most unique and fun hostels. It is inside the Rossio train station in the central and historic Baixa area. The hostel has 28 rooms, including private and dorm-style accommodations. Each room is uniquely adorned with creative accents and furnished with all the necessities. In addition, there is a garden, a lounge, a bar, and a shared kitchen at the hostel. Along with various events and activities, including yoga classes, movie evenings, and karaoke nights, the hostel provides a warm and welcoming atmosphere. Dorm beds might cost anything from €15 to €25 per night.

LISBON INSIDER TIPS

Lisbon is a city full of hidden gems and surprises that are often difficult to locate or reach. Lisbon has many undiscovered attractions and insider knowledge that may enhance and personalize your vacation. Here are a few insider suggestions from Lisbon:

Visit the Carmo Convent: This is one of Lisbon's most fascinating and mysterious places and a hidden gem for any history and architecture lover. This 14th-century monastery was reduced to ashes after the 1755 earthquake largely destroyed it. It is now a museum with various objects, sculptures, and tombs from many eras and architectural styles. The magnificent Gothic nave of the monastery has columns, arches, and a skylight. Tickets cost €5, and the convent is open from 10:00 to 18:00 Monday through Saturday.

Take a Boat to Cacilhas: For everyone who likes the outdoors and adventure, this is one of the most picturesque and tranquil ways to enjoy the river and escape the city. You may cross the Tagus River by boat from the Cais do Sodré station to the Cacilhas station. The ten-minute boat trip provides a stunning perspective of the city and the bridge. You may also visit the Cacilhas region, which has some of the greatest vistas, including the Cristo Rei monument, and some of the best seafood restaurants, such as Ponto Final. The ferry costs €1.30 per ticket and operates daily from 05:30 to 01:30.

Discover the LX Factory: One of Lisbon's most innovative and cultural centers, it's a must-visit for anybody who appreciates art and design. It was formerly an industrial complex transformed into a colorful, diverse area with plenty of street art, stores, cafés, and eateries. In addition to a massive mural of a woman's face by Brazilian artist Vhils, there is a plethora of street art with various styles and meanings painted on the walls, rooftops, and floors. Additionally, you may visit some stores, such as Wish, a concept store with a range of goods and services, and Ler

Devagar, a bookshop with a flying bike. The LX Factory is free to enter and is open daily from 6:00 to 04:00.

Attend a Fado Performance at Clube de Fado: The fado, a traditional and heartfelt Lisbon music recognized as a UNESCO Intangible Cultural Heritage, may be heard in one of the most genuine and moving settings. It's a club near the Sé Cathedral in the charming and ancient Alfama neighborhood. Every night, the club has a live fado concert where you can experience the passion and melancholy of the genre while listening to some of the greatest singers and guitarists in the city. Along with a selection of wines and beverages, the club offers a delectable and traditional menu centered on Portuguese and Mediterranean cuisine. The club is open daily from 20:00 to 2:00. A customer may expect to pay between €40 and €60, which includes supper and a performance.

LISBON CULTURAL TIPS

Lisbon's rich and varied history and culture reflect its multicultural and maritime background. In addition to appreciating some of the city's most striking and significant features, you may learn much about Lisbon's and Portugal's culture and history. Here are some cultural pointers for Lisbon:

Pick up a few Portuguese Expressions and Words: Portuguese is a lovely and expressive language that serves as Lisbon and Portugal's primary language. You may demonstrate respect and interest in the local people and culture by learning Portuguese terms and phrases to help communicate and interact with them. The following are a few Portuguese words and phrases:

Olá: Hello

Bom dia: Good morning

Boa tarde: Good afternoon

Boa noite: Good evening/night

Obrigado/Obrigada: Thank you (male/female)

De nada: You're welcome

Desculpe: Sorry/Excuse me

Sim/Não: Yes/No

Por favor: Please

Quanto custa?: How much is it

Onde fica?Where is it?

Como se chama?: What is your name?

Prazer em conhecê-lo/a: Nice to meet you (male/female)

Fala inglês?: Do you speak English?

Não falo português: I don't speak Portuguese

Visit the Cultural and Historical Attractions:
Lisbon has a lot of cultural and historical attractions that showcase the history and the identity of Lisbon and Portugal and offer a lot of art and beauty. You may take in some of the city's most striking and significant features, explore some of the historical and cultural sites, and learn more about the history, present, and future of the nation and the city. Here are some of the historical and cultural attractions:

Museu Nacional de Arte Antiga: This is the national museum of ancient art and one of Lisbon's most important and visited museums. It showcases various ornamental arts, paintings, and sculptures from Portugal and other nations, including Spain, France, Italy, and the Netherlands, spanning the 12th to the 19th centuries. The museum has a garden with views of the bridge and river. The museum is open

Tuesday through Sunday from 10:00 to 18:00. Tickets are €6.

Padrão dos Descobrimentos: This is a monument to the discoveries and one of Lisbon's most iconic and symbolic landmarks. The sculpture, which stands 52 meters tall and resembles a ship, is embellished with sculptures of artists, rulers, and explorers who contributed to Portuguese colonial and marine exploration. In addition, the monument has a theater, an exhibition hall, and a lookout that overlooks the tower and the river. The memorial is accessible Tuesday through Sunday from 10:00 to 18:00. Tickets are €6.

Teatro Nacional de São Carlos: This is the national theater of São Carlos and one of Lisbon's most elegant and prestigious venues. Built in the neoclassical style in the eighteenth century, this theater is devoted to classical music and opera. Together with a museum showcasing various costumes, instruments, and artifacts, the theater offers a rich and diverse program featuring national and international artists and performers. Tickets cost €5, and the theater is open from 10:00 to 17:00 Monday through Friday.

Enjoy the Local Festivals and Events: Lisbon has a lot of local festivals and events that celebrate the culture and traditions of Lisbon and Portugal and offer a lot of fun and entertainment. You may participate in some of the community's festivals and events, feel the joy and energy of the people and the city, and join the residents in their celebrations. Among the celebrations and activities in the area are:

Festas de Lisboa: This month-long celebration of the city and Santo António, its patron saint, is Lisbon's primary event. June is the festival's month, offering various events and activities, including street parties, concerts, parades, and fairs. The customary sardine BBQ, the vibrant paper decorations, and the basil plants—presented as a sign of friendship and love—are all event elements. The event, which is free and accessible to everyone, is held around the city in several districts, including Graça, Bairro Alto, and Alfama.

Rock in Rio Lisboa: This is one of the biggest and most popular music festivals in Lisbon and the world. This biannual event, which happens in May or June, brings together some of the greatest and most well-known performers and bands from various genres, including rock, pop, hip-hop, and electronic. Entertainment and activities, including rides, games, stores, and food vendors, are also available during the event. Tickets for the event cost between €69 and €117, depending on the day and the lineup. It is held in the Parque da Bela Vista.

Noite Branca: This is one of Lisbon's most magical and enchanting events and a night to remember. It is a yearly festival in September and includes various artistic and cultural manifestations, including theater, dance, music, and film. The city and the monuments are illuminated and decorated by the event's abundance of lights and colors. The event, which is free and accessible to everyone, is held around the city in a variety of locations, including Baixa, Chiado, and Belém.

CHAPTER NINE

BEST DAY TRIPS FROM LISBON (BY A LOCAL!)

Lisbon is a bustling city with much to do, but it's also an ideal place to begin to visit some of the surrounding spots for a unique and complementary experience. Several-day excursions from Lisbon are both simple and quick to go there by car or public transit, and they will enhance both your vacation and your understanding of Portugal. As recommended by locals, these are some of the top day excursions from Lisbon:

Sintra: This is one of Portugal's most magical and enchanting places and a UNESCO World Heritage Site. This town, which is around 30 km west of Lisbon, is well-known for its fanciful castles, palaces, and gardens that evoke the history and culture of Portugal while also providing an abundance of artistic and picturesque features. The Pena Palace, Quinta da Regaleira, Moorish Castle, and Monserrate Palace are some of Sintra's most notable and well-visited landmarks. Along with tasting some of the specialties from the area, such as queijadas and traversers, you may take in the natural surroundings, the town's vistas, and the sea. The train from the Rossio station takes around 40 minutes to reach Sintra and a round-trip ticket costs €4.50. The daily hours of operation for the attractions are 09:30 to 18:00, with admission prices varying according to the kind of attraction.

Cascais: This is one of the most charming and relaxing places in Portugal and a popular seaside resort. This town, which is around 30 km west of Lisbon, is well-known for its beaches, marina, and fortifications, all of which provide plenty of fun activities in addition to plenty of sun and sea. The natural rock formation known as Boca do Inferno, the museum dedicated to Portuguese painter Paula Rego, the Farol de Santa Marta, which is both a lighthouse and a museum, the Parque Marechal Carmona, which is a park featuring a lake and a playground, are some of the most appealing and popular attractions in Cascais. In addition, you may explore some neighboring locations, such as Guincho and Estoril, and take advantage of the local nightlife and food. Train travel to Cascais from the Cais do Sodré station takes around forty minutes, and the cost is €4.50 return. Depending on the attraction, tickets might cost anywhere from €3 to €5. The attractions are open daily from 10:00 to 18:00.

Óbidos: This is a medieval gem and one of Portugal's most picturesque and romantic places. Around 80 kilometers north of Lisbon, this town is well-known for its walls, castles, and churches, all providing a wealth of historical and cultural significance while retaining their old beauty. The Porta da Vila, a gate with a tiled chapel; the Castelo de Óbidos, a castle, and hotel; the Igreja de Santa Maria, a painted-ceilinged church; and the Aqueduto da

Usseira, an aqueduct, and viewpoint are a few of the most fascinating and well-visited sites in Óbidos. Aside from tasting some of the regional delicacies, such as pão-de-ló, a sponge cake, and ginjinha, a cherry liqueur, you can also take part in the festivals and events held in the area, including the chocolate festival, the medieval market, and the Christmas village. The bus from the Campo Grande station takes around an hour to reach Óbidos, and the cost is €8 return. Depending on the attraction, tickets might cost anywhere from €2 to €6. The attractions are open daily from 09:00 to 18:00.

BEST MUSEUMS IN LISBON

Lisbon is home to many museums that provide a wealth of information and amusement while showcasing the history, culture, and character of Lisbon and Portugal. Lisbon has many museums that appeal to a wide range of interests and inclinations and include a wide range of collections and exhibitions, from local to international, ancient to contemporary. The following are a few of Lisbon's top museums:

Museu Nacional do Azulejo: This is the national museum of the azulejo, the traditional and colorful tile that decorates many of the buildings and walls in Lisbon. The museum has a collection of tiles from Portugal and other nations, including Spain, France, Italy, and the Netherlands, spanning many eras and styles from the 15th to the 20th century. The museum also has a café with views of the river and bridge and a workshop where you may create your tiles. The museum costs €5 per entry and is open from 10:00 to 18:00 every Tuesday through Sunday.

Museu Calouste Gulbenkian: This is one of the most prestigious and comprehensive museums in Lisbon and one of the most visited museums in Portugal. It showcases a selection of pieces by some of the most well-known and significant painters from many genres and periods, including Rodin, Monet, Renoir, and Rembrandt. In addition, the museum has a performance hall, a library, a contemporary art center, and a park. The museum is open from 10:00 to 18:00 on Wednesday through Monday. Tickets cost €12.50, which includes admission to the contemporary art center.

Museu do Fado: One of Lisbon's most poignant and cultural museums, this one is a must-see for fans of Portuguese music. It is a UNESCO Intangible Cultural Heritage and a museum devoted to the fado, Lisbon's traditional and soulful music. The museum presents the fado's history and development through displays, instruments, and recordings. Every day, the museum hosts a live fado concert, including some of the top guitarists and vocalists in the city. The museum costs €5 per entry and is open from 10:00 to 18:00 every Tuesday through Sunday.

CHAPTER TEN

7 DAYS IN LISBON: THE PERFECT LISBON ITINERARY FOR FIRST-TIME VISITORS

Lisbon is a city that offers a lot of attractions and activities for any taste and interest. Without getting tired or hurried, you can spend a week in Lisbon and see the greatest parts of the city and its surroundings. For those who are visiting Lisbon for the first time, the following itinerary will help you make the most of your seven days there:

Day 1: Discover the Baixa and Chiado Districts

Begin your day in Lisbon's main entrance, the Praça do Comércio, the city's most stately and spectacular plaza. See the Arco da Rua Augusta, a colossal arch with a viewpoint, and take in the architecture and river vistas. The arch costs €3 per ticket and is available daily from 9:00 to 19:00.

Stroll along the main pedestrian street in the Baixa neighborhood, Rua Augusta, and take in the boutiques, cafés, and street entertainers. Visit the Elevador de Santa Justa, a 19th-century elevator that links the Chiado and Baixa neighborhoods and provides a sweeping perspective of the city. The lift is available daily from 7:00 to 23:00, with tickets costing €5.50, including access to the viewpoint.

Proceed to the Rossio, Lisbon's busiest and most important area, where you may take in the mosaic floor, the monument, and the fountain. See the neoclassical theater and museum, Teatro Nacional D. Maria II, and the stunning and ancient Rossio rail station. Tickets cost €5, and the theater is open Tuesday through Sunday from 10:00 to 18:00.

Stroll up to the Largo do Carmo, a quaint and serene plaza, and visit the 14th-century monastery that was reduced to ruins after being largely damaged by an earthquake in 1755. It is now a museum with various objects, sculptures, and tombs from many eras and architectural styles. Tickets cost €5, and the convent is open from 10:00 to 18:00 Monday through Saturday.

By crossing the street, enjoy the stores, cafés, restaurants, and museums in the Chiado neighborhood, Lisbon's historical and cultural center. See the modern and contemporary art museum, Museu Nacional de Arte Contemporânea do Chiado, and the 16th-century church, Igreja de São Roque, which has an opulent interior. The church is free to enter and is open daily from 9:30 to 17:00. The museum is open from 10:00 to 18:00 on Wednesday through Monday. Tickets are €4.50 each.

Take the city and river views from Lisbon's most romantic and expansive viewpoint, the Miradouro de São Pedro de Alcântara, as you round off your day here. You may also enjoy the ambiance and music at the kiosk while having a drink or a snack.

Day 2: Explore the Alfama and Castelo Districts

The oldest and most significant cathedral in Lisbon and a representation of the history and character of the city, the Sé Cathedral is a great place to start the day. It was constructed in the twelfth century and has a fortress-like aspect, combining Gothic and Romanesque architectural elements. The cathedral's admission is free and open daily from 9:00 to 19:00.

Journey to the Castelo de São Jorge, Lisbon's most historic and picturesque landmark that is a must-see for all travelers. This ancient fortress is perched atop the city's tallest hill, with a commanding view of Alfama and Baixa neighborhoods. The castle's history is lengthy and tumultuous, spanning the Roman, Moorish, and Christian eras. The ticket cost is €10, and the castle is accessible daily from 9:00 to 21:00.

Stroll down to the Miradouro de Santa Luzia, a popular destination for inhabitants and visitors, which is one of Lisbon's most exquisite and charming perspectives. It provides a breathtaking view of the National Pantheon's dome, the river, and the roofs. The vantage point has a fountain, a pergola, and a tiled wall. The vantage point is free to enter and open daily from 8:00 to 0:00.

Proceed to the Alfama neighborhood, Lisbon's most historic and scenic location, to see the real, traditional side of the city. The neighborhood is distinguished by its colorful homes, meandering lanes, and breathtaking hilltop vistas. Some of the most significant structures, including the National Pantheon, the Fado Museum, and the São Vicente de Fora Church, are also located there. The church is open daily from 10:00 to 18:00, with tickets costing €5. The Pantheon is open Tuesday through Sunday from 10:00 to

17:00. Tickets cost €4. The museum costs €5 per entry and is available from 10:00 to 18:00 every Tuesday through Sunday.

The oldest and most well-known flea market in Lisbon, Feira da Ladra, is a wonderful spot to end your day and discover some excellent finds and deals. Various items, including clothing, jewelry, crafts, antiques, literature, and street performers, are available. The market is free to enter and is open Tuesday through Saturday from 9:00 to 18:00.

Day 3: Explore the Neighborhoods of Belém and Alcântara

Begin your day with the Mosteiro dos Jerónimos, a UNESCO World Heritage Site, and Lisbon's most spectacular structure. Constructed in the Manueline style during the 16th century, the monastery is devoted to the Order of Saint Jerome. In addition, the royal family and explorers like Vasco da Gama and Luís de Camões were buried there. Tickets are €10, and the monastery is open Tuesday through Sunday from 10:00 to 17:00.

Stroll to the Padrão dos Descobrimentos, one of Lisbon's most recognizable and significant sites and a memorial to the discoveries. The sculpture, which stands 52 meters tall and resembles a ship, is embellished with sculptures of artists, rulers, and explorers who contributed to Portuguese colonial and marine exploration. In addition, the monument has a theater, an exhibition hall, and a lookout that overlooks the tower and the river. The memorial is accessible Tuesday through Sunday from 10:00 to 18:00. Tickets are €6.

Stroll to the Torre de Belém, a UNESCO World Heritage Site and Lisbon's most famous and significant structure. Built in the Manueline style in the sixteenth century, the tower is embellished with religious and marine themes. It was once a ceremonial and defensive building that served as a jail and a customs house. The tower is accessible Tuesday through Sunday from 10:00 to 17:00. A ticket is €6.

Stroll to the Pastéis de Belém, Lisbon's most well-known and delectable pastry shop—if not the globe. The pastel de nata is a tiny, round custard tart with a crispy, flaky crust, a creamy, sweet center, and a dusting of sugar and cinnamon. It is the original and only spot to sample it. It was created in the eighteenth century by the monks of Jerónimos Monastery, and the family recipe is being used today. The price per tart is €1.20, and the store is open daily from 8:00 to 23:00.

Take a tram or a bus to Lisbon's Alcântara district. This historical and cultural area is home to some of the city's most striking and iconic monuments, including the Cristo Rei, a Christ statue modeled after Christ the Redeemer, and the 25 de Abril Bridge, a suspension bridge resembling the Golden Gate Bridge. The bridge is open daily from 10:00 to 18:00, with tickets costing €6. The statue is available for $5 per ticket and is open daily from 9:30 to 18:30.

The LX Factory, a former industrial complex transformed into a creative and cultural center with many street art, boutiques, cafés, and restaurants, is a great place to end the day. In addition to a massive mural of a woman's face by Brazilian artist Vhils, there is a plethora of street art with various styles and meanings painted on the walls, rooftops, and floors. Additionally, you may visit some stores, such as Wish, a concept store with a range of goods and services, and Ler Devagar, a bookshop with a flying bike. The LX Factory is free to enter and is open daily from 6:00 to 04:00.

Day 4: Spend the Day in Sintra

Take a train for €4.50 for a round-trip ticket from the Rossio station to the Sintra station, which takes around 40 minutes.

The Pena Palace, a UNESCO World Heritage Site and Sintra's most charming and romantic sight is a great place to start your day. Built in the Romantic style in the 19th century, the palace is embellished with vibrant and exotic designs. It has a lot of beauty and art; it was the royal family's vacation home. The palace is open daily from 09:30 to 18:00, with tickets costing €14.

Stroll to the Quinta da Regaleira, a UNESCO World Heritage Site and one of Sintra's most enigmatic and captivating sights. This estate from the 20th century has a palace, a church, and a garden. It contains symbolism and mysteries about mythology, alchemy, and masonry. In addition, the estate has a system of wells and tunnels that lead to various floors and spaces. The estate is open daily from 09:30 to 18:00, with tickets costing €10.

The Moorish Castle, a UNESCO World Heritage Site and one of Sintra's oldest and most picturesque sights can be reached by bus or cab. The Moors constructed this stronghold in the tenth century, and the Christians eventually took control of it. It provides a broad perspective of the town and the sea and has a stormy and lengthy history. Tickets cost €8, and the castle is open daily from 09:30 to 18:00.

The Monserrate Palace, a UNESCO World Heritage Site and one of Sintra's most exquisite and striking sights may be reached by bus or cab. Built in the Orientalist style in the 19th century, the palace is embellished with Indian and Arabic designs. It has a lot of beauty and art, and it was the home of British billionaire Francis Cook. There is also a park at the palace, filled with many exotic flora and plants. Tickets cost €8, and the palace is open daily from 09:30 to 18:00.

Return to Lisbon by train and spend your last moments in the stunning and historic Restauradores Square, home to some of the greatest eateries and pubs in the city. Here, you can also take in the local atmosphere and nightlife.

Day 5: Spend the Day at Cascais

Take a train for €4.50 for a round-trip ticket from the Cais do Sodré station to the Cascais station. The ride takes around 40 minutes.

Begin your day at the Boca do Inferno, a naturally occurring rock formation with a view of the surf and cliffs that mimic the jaws of hell. Additionally, there are a few cafés and souvenir stores where you may purchase souvenirs and food. Every day from 8:00 to 20:00, the Boca do Inferno is open. Admission is free.

Stroll to one of Cascais's most cutting-edge and visually striking attractions, the Casa do Histórias Paula Rego, a museum honoring the Portuguese painter Paula Rego. It features a selection of the artist's paintings, which are well-known for their figurative and narrative styles and tackle subjects including politics, feminism, and sexuality. The museum also has a store, a café, and a garden. The museum is open Tuesday through Sunday from 10:00 to 18:00. Tickets are €3.

Stroll to the Farol de Santa Marta, a museum and lighthouse providing abundant culture and history, with plenty of sun and water. The lighthouse is still in service today, constructed in the 1800s. Various items and documentation about the technological advancements and historical background of lighthouses in Portugal are exhibited in the museum. The museum and lighthouse are open from 10:00 to 17:00, Wednesday through Monday. Tickets are €3.

Take a stroll to Parque Marechal Carmona, one of Cascais' most lovely and serene parks—a wonderful spot for leisure and a picnic. In addition to the many trees, flowers, and ponds in the park, there is a playground, a bandstand, and a café. In addition, the park has three worthwhile attractions: a church, a museum, and a library. Every day from 7:00 to 0:00, the park is open. There is no charge to enter.

You may stroll to the most well-liked and stunning beach in Cascais, Praia da Ribeira, which is a terrific spot to enjoy the sun, the water, and some fun and entertainment. The beach offers plenty of water, waves, and sand, including restrooms, sun loungers, and umbrellas. There are several eateries and bars along the beach where you can have a meal or a drink while enjoying the scenery and the music. The beach is free to enter and is accessible daily from 8:00 to 20:00.

Return to Lisbon by train and spend your last hours in Bairro Alto, the city's most vibrant and bustling nightlife district, with hundreds of clubs, pubs, and restaurants to suit all tastes and price ranges. You may enjoy the vistas and the street art in this laid-back and welcoming location while drinking, chatting, and mingling with residents and visitors. The area is open daily from 18:00 until 2:00, with drinks priced between €1 and €5.

Day 6: Take a Day Trip to Óbidos

Buses cost €8 for a round-trip ticket from the Campo Grande station to Óbidos station, which takes around one hour.

Begin your day at Óbidos' main gate, Porta da Vila, which is also one of the town's most beautiful and scenic sights. It has a balcony overlooking the wall and the street and a tiled chapel dedicated to Our Lady of Mercy. The gate is open daily from 9:00 to 18:00, and free admission.

As you stroll, enjoy the stores, cafés, and galleries along Rua Direita, the town's main thoroughfare. You can purchase souvenirs and local delicacies, including pão-de-ló, a sponge cake, and ginjinha, a cherry liqueur. The street is free to enter and is accessible daily from 9:00 to 18:00.

Stroll to the UNESCO World Heritage Site, Castelo de Óbidos, the city's most striking and prominent feature. The Moors constructed this stronghold in the twelfth century, and the

Christians eventually took control of it. It provides a broad perspective of the town and surrounding region and has a long, stormy past. You may stay at the castle and take in the ambiance of the Middle Ages since it doubles as a hotel. Tickets cost €6, and the castle is open daily from 09:00 to 18:00.

Stroll to the Igreja de Santa Maria, Ñbidos's most significant and oldest church and a representation of the town's past and present. It was constructed in the twelfth century and has a fortress-like aspect, combining Gothic and Romanesque architectural elements. The church's interior is opulent and ornate, with a Renaissance tomb, a baroque altar, and a painted ceiling. The church is free to enter and is open daily from 9:00 to 18:00.

Stroll to the Aqueduto da Usseira, an aqueduct, and viewpoint that provides abundant sun, sky, and natural heritage. The aqueduct is three kilometers long and eighteen meters high. It was constructed in the sixteenth century. There is a lookout on the aqueduct from which you may view the town and the sea. The aqueduct is free to enter and is accessible daily from 9:00 to 18:00.

Return to Lisbon by bus, and spend your last moments there in the sophisticated and lovely Praça do Príncipe Real, home to some of the top eateries and pubs in the city. Here, you can also take in the local ambiance and nightlife.

Day 7: Enjoy Your Last Day in Lisbon

Visit the Museu Nacional do Azulejo, the national museum dedicated to the traditional and vibrant tile known as "azulejo," which adorns several walls and buildings in Lisbon, to start your day. The museum has a collection of tiles from Portugal and other nations, including Spain, France, Italy, and the Netherlands, spanning many eras and styles from the 15th to the 20th century. The museum also has a café with views of the river and bridge and a workshop where you may create your tiles. The museum costs €5 per entry and is open from 10:00 to 18:00 every Tuesday through Sunday.

To go to the most futuristic and contemporary part of Lisbon, Parque das Nações, where Expo 98, a global exposition honoring the 500th anniversary of Portuguese discoveries, was held, take a bus or a cab. The biggest aquarium in Europe, Oceanário, a science and technology museum, a cable car that gives a panoramic view of the neighborhood, the Teleférico, a gambling and entertainment venue, and the Casino Lisboa are just a few of the many sights and activities available in the area. The region has many stores, cafés, restaurants, and green areas. The Oceanário costs €19 per ticket and is open daily from 10:00 to 19:00. Tickets for the Pavilhão do Conhecimento cost €9 and are available Tuesday through Friday from 10:00 to 18:00 and on Saturday and Sunday from 11:00 to 19:00. The Teleférico ticket costs €4 and is available every day from 11:00 to 19:00. Every day from 15:00 to 03:00, the Casino Lisboa is open. Admission is free.

The most attractive and prominent boulevard in Lisbon, Avenida da Liberdade, is a terrific spot to promenade and shop. You may get there by bus or metro. The road is lined with abundant stores, hotels, theaters, and monuments, including the Marquês de Pombal statue of the prime minister who oversaw the city's reconstruction after the 1755 earthquake and the Monumento aos Mortos da Grande Guerra, a monument honoring those who lost their lives in World War I. In addition, the avenue has a pedestrian promenade in the center and several trees, fountains, and sculptures. The avenue is free to enter and is accessible daily from 8:00 to 22:00.

Take in the city and the sunset from one of Lisbon's most beautiful and tranquil vantage points, the Miradouro da Graça, as you wind down your day. You may also enjoy the ambiance and music at the kiosk while having a drink or a snack. The vantage point is free to enter and open daily from 8:00 to 0:00.

CHAPTER ELEVEN

LISBON TRAVEL TIPS AND TRICKS
FROM A LOCAL

Lisbon has many activities and attractions to suit every interest and taste. Additionally, the city offers a wealth of advice to make travel more accessible and pleasurable. Here are some insider travel advice and recommendations for Lisbon for 2024 from a local:

Use the Lisboa Card: This card allows you to use public transit, such as the metro, buses, trams, and trains, for free or at a reduced rate. It also grants you entry to over 80 attractions, museums, and monuments in Lisbon. The card is available for purchase online or in person at the tourist office, with choices for 24, 48, or 72 hours. Depending on how much you use, you may save up to €100 with the card, which costs €22, €38, or €48, accordingly.

Stay Clear of the Busy Season: June through August is the busiest time of year to visit Lisbon, which is also one of the most popular. Visit Lisbon between September and May, when things are less crowded, lines move more quickly, and costs are lower. With an average temperature of 18°C, you may take advantage of a more agreeable, laid-back attitude and milder, sunny weather.

Make Reservations For Your Lodging In Advance: Many different types of lodging are available in Lisbon, including hotels, hostels, and guesthouses. However, there is a great demand for accommodation in Lisbon and a limited supply, particularly in the historic and central districts of Baixa, Chiado, and Alfama. You should reserve your lodging well in advance, ideally one month before your trip, to locate a decent and affordable place to stay. To identify and evaluate the most incredible offers and discounts for your lodging, utilize the Bing search engine.

Use Public Transportation: The majority of Lisbon and its environs are serviced by Lisbon's excellent and effective public transportation system. The city's significant regions, attractions, and neighboring locations like Sintra, Cascais, and Ñbidos may be reached by rail, bus, tram, and metro. Purchasing a single ticket, a day pass or a rechargeable card is an option based on your requirements and tastes. Planning your public transportation routes and timetables is another way to use the Bing maps.

Try the Local Foods and Drinks: Lisbon offers a wide variety of locally produced foods and drinks that provide a lot of flavor and diversity and represent the history and culture of Lisbon and Portugal. You may sample some of the regional fare, including the grilled sardine called sardinha, the custard dessert called pastel de nata, and the salted cod fish called bacalhau. A few regional beverages are also available, such as the ginjinha, a cherry liqueur; the café, a robust and fragrant coffee; and the vinho verde, a green wine. Numerous inexpensive and locally owned dining establishments exist throughout the city's several districts, including Alfama, Bairro Alto, and Mouraria.

Learn Some Portuguese Terms and Expressions: Portuguese is a lovely and expressive language, and Lisbon is Portugal's official and primary language. Acquiring a few Portuguese words and phrases to facilitate your interactions and communication with the locals while demonstrating your interest in and respect for their way of life is possible.

CONCLUSION

Everybody can find something to do in Lisbon. You may discover everything in this dynamic and sunny city, including history, culture, nightlife, beaches, and food. With its gorgeous neighborhoods, breathtaking vistas, and welcoming people, Lisbon is a city that never ceases to amaze me. You're welcome to explore, discover, and have fun in Lisbon.

This book teaches you about the top destinations and activities and advises you to make the most of your vacation. Furthermore, you now possess knowledge of this intriguing city's history, customs, and culture. Lisbon has transformed throughout the ages, going from a Phoenician settlement to a major worldwide city, all while maintaining its unique character and cultural legacy.

However, Lisbon and its environs still have a plethora of other sights and activities to offer. If you have more time, you may explore the spectacular beaches along the Atlantic coast, the historic sites of Évora and Óbidos, and the charming villages of Sintra and Cascais. As a base, Lisbon allows you to visit other parts of Portugal, including the Azores, the Douro Valley, and the Algarve. This varied and stunning nation offers an endless array of alternatives.

We hope this book has been enjoyable and encouraged you to visit Lisbon in 2024. We're sure you will adore this city as much as we did. Have a fantastic trip in Lisbon, and thanks for selecting our tour guide!

Printed in Great Britain
by Amazon

44154548R00086